For all of the hopeless souls reading my poems; your words will come with time. Be vibrant, be bold, and don't be afraid to fall.

Thank you to my dear friends for their encouragement in the times I was unsure of myself.

For mom, dad, and Logan. You all loved me when no one else could.

Coloured Ink

Table of Contents

Part I; The Reds

Part II; The Blues

Part III; The Greens

Could it be that we are nothing but coloured ink? The way we draw ourselves, the delicate lines of our thoughts, each are surrounded by the fragile hues of humanity. Our present is paper, our choices the pen. Choose your tones wisely, for someday the quill will run dry.

Coloured Ink

The Reds

Our hearts shine scarlet against the silent tones of humanity. Love; it was a mysterious thing neither of us had grown used to just yet, but it didn't stop coursing through our veins. Each of us may break, or we could mold into one, as if two was a number we'd not existed as ever before.

Scarlet

One day, I'll be able to notice
beautiful boys without falling for them.
I'll admire their eyes and the way their hair
swoops across their faces without feeling
the familiarity of love cascading past me.
On this momentous day, reality will separate
from my over-committed daydreams.
Naivety will be a foreign concept, and sense
will take its place.
Today is not that day.
Today, I see your tired, honey eyes, the flatness
of your voice, and I wonder what you're listening
to.
And I wonder if you know just how lovely you are.

Beautiful boys

In the softest, pinkest hour of day, I find my mind wandering to thoughts of you. The ones I held hostage from breakfast's daydreams and hopeful steps down the hall.

My evening consists of you.

Your sentences swim in magenta tea, the way your eyes catch mine hidden in the fabric of my sheets. Warmth floods my cheeks when your fingers lace through mine, even now, as they ache awaiting your return.

Your kindness floats in the sunset's reflection. Though I long for daybreak, when you sit quietly beside me, your memories keep me company.

The Sunset's Reflection

Have you ever really looked at him?
The scars on his cheeks and the way he
runs his fingers through his hair?
He is extraordinary in every move he makes.
He is stunning in every light of day.
The warm September breeze reminds me of you.
So delicate, but it's presence is never
ignored, never neglected.
Though he sits three feet away,
I've never been closer to him.
On this day, in the plastic chair and
tapping at keys till my fingers become raw,
I've found my home.

Don't let september end

His eyes still smiled, even when he wore a frown like his favourite pair of shoes.

Mopey

The two of us are benign.
Love has never sent us sprawling through
life with carelessness and spontaneity,
it has never adorned the neatly combed hair
atop our heads.
We are peaceful in our uniformity,
calculating our regrets to figure out where we went wrong.
If two people were as perfectly square as we are-
wittiness as sharp as it gets, measured movements
carrying us through even the most mellow of days-
they could never see past the comfort of their own skins.
Not us.
I know that my sweet, intelligent boy and I
will never amount to anything.
We will be consistent glances across the table
and shared knowledge, but we will never be in love.
For once, I am grateful for a boy I am certain
will never know me.
He is made from the shallow salad days
I think I needed during this dreadful winter.

Salad days

My love, just whisper it to me. How do you feel about me today? Your dark eyes shine so bright in contrast with the tan glow of your complexion. Wouldn't it be so lovely if your lips brushed mine! How would you like the breeze against your neck as we walk along the sea, hand-in-hand? If I were a flower, would you pick me? Am I who you would choose?

Vivid Daydreaming

I've never been fond of Tuesdays.
The dreary, sunken faces of students
itching to make it through another class,
another day, kept alive only by thoughts of the weekend.

t wasn't until the last Tuesday of October,
when I woke up to your message,
that Tuesdays didn't seem so sad and frightening.

Every hour, I'd check for a reply,
comforted by the fact that, god, you really just might. I don't know how you could, or why you would, but you may.

It's funny how detest does that,
it fades when you peel back it's layers,
questioning if your logic could be false, if there's another way.

With you, there was.

The anger that rose in my chest when you brushed past, asking how I was, what I'd done that day, acting so perfectly normal.

Nowadays I can't seem to get you out of my head,
your charming demeanor taking place of the distaste
that once lived there so contently.
I
 didn't want to feel this way.

I screamed and cried and submerged myself deep in
the greenery of the forest to forget you, but
somehow, somewhere along the way,
you have mastered the art of winning people over.

How can I resist, when your blond hair falls so
peacefully across your face, warm hands all over
me, and that smile, dear god, that smile.

The answer is, I couldn't resist,
so now you have made me fall in love with
Tuesdays, simply because they've proven that hope
is reachable.

Tuesday's are for the heart

Loving him was honey dripping from a spoon. It started slowly, but if I'd blinked? Oh, had my eyes closed, I would have missed it.

The Bee's Knees

The old navy blue car taught us things about each other words never could have. *Kiss me*, my mind pleaded. *Forget her, kiss me.* But just friends, we've always been! Coffee did not mean we could be together, no sir. Did I ever wish you would just lean in…..

forbidden fruit

You are the days that I stand in the mirror, wondering if the shape of my thighs, the waves in my hair, the words that I write are not good enough for you. You are the thoughts that consume me in my most vulnerable hour. And you are the voice that silences them.

Differing Opinions

I don't want to lie about you.
If only you'd know that I feel the same,
that the glances of admiration you throw at me are
returned, and at night you are the one I think about.
I dreamt of you.
We couldn't help but lace our fingers together
and sitting two feet apart didn't cause our knees to
shake and crumble.
You could so easily be the boy plastered all over my
medias.
We could be so happy, content in our mellow
mindsets.
I imagine going to the art gallery,
your arm around my waist, in a place where silence
is productive.
I love the way your face falls and lifts itself
when I walk into a room.
Just know that my stomach is doing the same thing,
at the same time.
My sweet boy, look me in the eyes. Tell me what
you need to.
I'm not going anywhere.

Muted love

Love, did you know that you look best in red? Deep, bright red, like a fire truck on a cloudy day. Your dark eyes seem brighter somehow, as if you fit into your pale complexion. Yes, red, it suits you.

Crimson

Hey there, green eyes. Won't you stay a while? I know we could never, but should we ever? Oh, should I let myself, I may fall in love with you. Waves would crash upon the shores and the sun may appear from behind the clouds, the stars could align just to tell us that this is not a bad thing. The moon does not frown at us as we sit across from each other, hearts in our throats, deeply immersed in the moment. If there is not a sign, not four seconds of peace, than maybe I'll risk it. Maybe I'll tell you today.

This Afternoon's Recollections

Her words were effortless, he could tell it by looking at the delicate cursive sprawled across her page. Her dry humour made the beige walls seem a little more colourful than they were the day before, and her eyes were the deepest green, the colour of pine in late autumn. Maybe she would look his way?

Symmetry, Part 1

Whenever she spoke, she could feel his eyes tracing her. Last Friday, he had smiled as soon as she littered her words into the air, quick as her voice filled the room. She remembered how the sunlight seemed to get caught in his curls, turning them golden. Do you think he's looking her way?

Symmetry, Part 2

Love, unravel me, piece by piece, until no layers remain between us. Shatter me till there's nothing left but an aching emptiness wringing throughout my skin and my heart screams for you to come back. I want you, for a beautiful mess is what's we'd be.

A beautiful mess

He would cross a million oceans to prove
that she was worth more than the boys
who'd only reluctantly jump puddles please
to her.

An ocean away

She was a girl who thrived off of sunlight. Flowers bloomed when she crossed a threshold, the radiance of a warm day threw itself upon her skin. He noticed how the dull fluorescence of artificial lighting may pass off as daylight when it fell onto her curls.

But there was a darkness to her forest eyes that intrigued him. What if she was a brick painted by nature? Could she be like him? A boy who loved to play acoustic guitar and wore dark-rimmed glasses that added to his broken disposition.

Could she love a boy whose face shone scarlet when her muted smile flashed in his direction? Would his hurried writing appear beside her careful words?

He crossed her and dotted her i's with a genuine love she'd never believed in.

Their colour pallet mixed so seamlessly. Adoration rose to the surface of her thoughts until nothing remained but him. And he loved her, too.

Differences Alike

The Blues

A church filled with flowers and black linen meant no else than a sorrowful morning. They lowered you into the ground, but your heart was still in pieces, attached to each and every colleague. He took you too soon, too young, too kind.

Megan

Where have you been? My voice is trapped, stinging my lips, warning me not to speak.
Are you angry with me? Heart beating too fast, oxygen drained from the room. You can't see the circles under my eyes, the fingers down my throat. How could you, when I've hid it so well, disguised sorrow as the plague?
I think we need space. Space. The phenomenon that leaves me awake during the quiet hours of morning, eyes closed during our afternoon plans. The very thing that stands over my pale body and laughs, kicking up dust on its' way out the door. Never opens, always closes.

Broken companionship

Sometimes I wonder why, after all this time, I've stayed by your side. Maybe it's the memories I've attached to your presence, or maybe it's that you knew me better than I knew myself.

The days of dialing your phone number, of numerous messages unrecognized, the constant need to make sure you hadn't done the unspeakable? They are over, my dear friend.

I do not hold feelings of distaste for you; I don't know that I ever could. But any quivering hopes of the your past self resurfacing have dwindled, and your demoralized shell sits before me now.

Less than human

A lifetime is seven days.
Four more have passed wordlessly,
messages from so many, but not you.
My patience has gone, my eggs returned
with a mournful glance as I walk away from you.
The kitchen light has gone out, and the
neon grocery lighting has taken its place.
I don't know if I want him, because how can
I think about love when you reached inside me
and snapped the strings of my heart with
those dark eyes and shallow looks.
I should choose him, I know it.
But why is it your name that floats around
my head in the weariness of midnight?

Don't do this to me

Corrupted by nausea,
sprinkled with anxiousness,
and drowned in affection.

These are the things I felt when you walked in,
that cautious grin sprawled across your face.

I wonder how long it took you to convince
your hair to fall so perfectly atop your head,
whether or not you knew when you picked
my favourite of your shirts from the closet.

When you sat down, barely a foot away,
did you see my hands shaking?

Were you aware that I was watching you
take note of my polite words,
your eyes lingering on my lips just a little
longer than they should have.

Careful glances upwards met my eyes, and love, I
noticed you notice me.

Perhaps you'd always looked at me this way,
or maybe it was brand new.

When you left, eleven minutes after taking my
heart in your hands, my world fell apart.

The sky opened up, rain falling quickly and
desperately.

Sitting at the beach where I'd imagined this day so
many times, an unkindness of ravens danced
overhead.

I think they could see the devastation painted on my
skin, the tears rolling from ocean to ocean.
The birds knew better than you did, and to me,
that was the part that ripped my insides in half
and caused the sobs to erupt from my quiet body.

An unkindness of ravens

Even after all this time, it still hurts me to see you. Your voice still echoes through my mind on the day where the quiet sinks in. There's an emptiness in my aching chest these days, and I can't help but wonder if it's the place you once stood. Tell me now, do you think of me often?

Hollow

Some people are easier to write about
than others.
With him, a thousand words was nowhere
near enough and dictionaries would unravel when
he stepped into their presence.
His darkness consumed him,
and though he was the muse of my greatest work,
you are different.
You are a forest in autumn.
Bursting with colours, aching to tell me your
stories.
You are all blond waves and rosy cheeks,
warm hands and daydreams.
Although he was poems pouring from the
deepest parts of my subconscious,
you are the challenge that keeps me up at
night until your soft voice calls out in my
unconscious hours.
He may have been the pain I pleaded for,
but you are the happiness I didn't know I deserved.

Something new

The sun disappeared from the sky when you left. Windows and doors bolted so tightly, not even a breeze could creep in.

Yet I find myself so terrified of who might crawl through the cracks in the floorboards that I lay here, screaming for you to come home. How could you let me lose my sanity just so that you can enjoy a night off?

Tears stream down my cheeks and I wail into the darkness, begging and pleading and crying for someone, anyone, to save me.
Not from the night. Not from those who lurk in the shadows. From myself.

Abandonment Issues

Every day he grew more distant. The halls we used to walk side by side seemed unfamiliar when his eyes wouldn't meet mine. Hellos were unreturned, messages sat patiently for hours on end. He killed off the butterflies in my stomach one by one. He threw bricks at me and disguised them as pebbles.

Unrequited.

He is the fine line between affection and affliction.
A few letters out of place, and the fleeting
romance we could have had is out the window,
quicker than the sunset's reflection disappears
from the water's edge.
My sad, sorrowful boy, you are every love song
written by a broken soul, a heartthrob to none but
me.
The sunlight of early summer has passed,
and our October hopes are no more.

Change of seasons

My sense was blind when it came to you. Hopelessly waiting for the boy that never showed up, the one whose physique occupied my mind and drowned out the pain.

Honey, you were never the right choice. We are puzzle pieces that don't fit together, unharmonized in every move we make.

These thoughts, they didn't stop me from wanting you. From pouring my heart and patience and love into you. It turns out, though, that the boy I was certain I was meant for didn't really know me at all.

Painful Realizations

You were my most prized affliction.
Temporary pain and likeness and aversion.
A temporary solution to a problem we were
not a part of. Though we thrived off of
prejudice, I didn't expect you to join the
skeletons in my closet.

Short-term

Meet me where the turquoise ocean falls
delicately upon the shore.
It's been too long since I've seen you here,
my love. What has changed?
The sunken ink in your arm,
the same one that held the barrel to your
throat just months ago, it seems so full of life
and possibility as it rests next to mine.
My flustered mind is at peace.

Every worry, every thought vanished when
you looked at me with those green eyes.
You truly saw me as you leaned in.
The very second her sickly thin body flashed
across your mind, I could tell.
Muscles tightened, jaw clenched as if she'd
been peeking in the window.
Your shameful heart had decided,
and my name was not the one your bright
eyes whispered in that moment.
Heavy limbs fumbled to escape the rancid air.
Little did I know,
that would be the last time I'd let myself see you.

We must do this again sometime

To her, he was the teal tinge in the greyest of oceans. Her greatest memories and darkest sunshine lived inside him, pulling on her heart strings until she snapped.

Strings

How am I supposed to breathe now that you're gone?
How can an oxygen mask save me when all that you
are and all that we were was what filled my lungs,
pumped blood through my veins and made me grow?
I was small and you fertilized me until I sprouted
from the driest of soils.
I am more than you, more than us. Do not blame me
for loving another when all I asked
was that you loved me.

Under oxygenated

I want the boy whose eyes stay glued to
mine in the middle of day.
The eyes that watch me over the rim of his
computer, who stops what he's doing
when I pick up my phone.
One whose hatred I've disguised as lust,
those same eyes darting in every which way
just to avoid the sight of me.
I am sorry for intruding, my love.
What's yours is not mine.
Ours hearts have changed, and my name is
not written on yours anymore.

Wake me when it's over

Darling, he was never worth a second glance.

Single Take

Selfishness clouds your perspective.
We all struggle, we have bad days,
we break down.
Who cares about others when you can smirk
into the mirror, right? Fate dealt its hand years
ago, get over yourself.
Welcome to the real world, society doesn't pity
those who've never worked a day in their lives.
You ask, they answer. It's always been that way.
Though, when you leave this building, when the
hallways fall and high school can't protect you
anymore?
That's when you'll truly learn what the rest of us
have known all along.

Rude awakenings

I must say I'm disappointed, love. I truly thought I had done better with you. There are too many questions, and it appears neither of us have any answers.

Questionable

I love too much.
They come stumbling into my presence and all of the sudden I'm swept under a rug, cowering at the thought of yet another heartbreak. But time and time again, I crawl out of my shell. My heart becomes full of their every word and my lungs expand with the air they breathe, getting lost in their eyes.
I love too much.
The doubts creep in during the darkest, most dreadful of evenings.
I love too much.
I'm broken. He's shattered me and I will never be repaired, he's cracked me open and exposed my most fragile thoughts, he's *ruined* me.
I love too much.

A damaged cycle.

When did the sleep escape your eyes, my love?
You ask the same, I see, but my unconscious
hours are dedicated to you.
Months without rest pile on top of each other,
with no intention of stopping.
How can I look at you, notice the lines of
exhaustion and stress on your skin, and have it wake
my soul during its darkest hour?
I've become quite ill.
The minutes I could have used to rejuvenate my
mind did not get used properly.
I shake and shiver with discontent,
not knowing if you feel the same.
Billions of seconds, I could spend staring at
the sky with you. After all, you are everything dark
and dreary combined with the most effortless
contentment I've ever witnessed.
How is it that seeing you makes me feel all of these
things,
but to you I'm no more than a shallow face in a
classroom of distaste?

My illness

On days like these, I feel the greyest of blues. The colour surrounding the moments after life but before beyond, the numb lifelessness of a limp figure.

Glaucous

I don't care to know where you ended up.
Your journey concluded in a place whose air had never filled my lungs. A place where words were held captive until the ransom had been paid and truthfulness no longer mattered. Caution was thrown to the wind as we parted, years passed without a peep. If an escape was all you craved, maybe the sea carried you to a lost island, one that drifts carelessly among waves.
I don't care to know where you ended up, but I hope you are happy there.

Lost Islands

Do you ever wonder how the darkness in his eyes came to be? What cruelty injected itself into his veins and flicked the light out? He was a tulip, soft and pure as the spring. Now, as the dead of winter rages forward, he is a rose; the deepest hue of crimson you have ever seen. It is unsettling, the way that boy moves. He lurches towards grass and rips it from the root, tearing life apart in his cold fingertips. But yet, he plants flowers in his concreteness.
His love is as catastrophic as a thorn, but with it brings the most mesmerizing of likeness.

A rose

When he took that wallflower from the shadows
and planted her so carefully in the richest of soils,
no one thought to question it. But as the summer
began to fade and the air grew cold, so did he. He
left her in the dust of fallen trees, and it wasn't until
she had wilted that they realized his absence hurt
her more than his actions.

Wilted

Sometimes my mind takes back broken promises. It sews them back together until more chances are revealed, ready to make room for forgiveness. Bad days are always numbered, right? Their harsh words will replace themselves with kind ones if time allows it, don't they?
I should know by now to dip my toes in before jumping off the fucking cliff.

A good heart never wins

I think I always knew that words could break a heart, but you showed me that silence is lethal.

Misguided

The first day I picked up a book on my own, I flipped to the very last page. I remember feeling a sense of disloyalty to the author, wanting nothing more than to know how it would end. Ever since, whenever I see a body of words strewn together with care, I read the last sentence before any others. To know what I'm dealing with, to protect myself from what lay behind the conclusion, to understand. Maybe, after all this time, it's how I knew you'd leave. I've scanned enough goodbyes and 'the end's to realize how all stories finish. With either happiness or despair. Fulfillment or destruction. Me or her.
How did I know, simply from reading us backwards, that it wouldn't be me?

Backwards

Mumbled words under bitter breath can still be heard. I should know, all of the ones you uttered shot right through my veins until I had grown cold.

I thought we were friends

Your eyes trace me differently now. There's a loneliness to the way your gaze catches mine, and I bet you wish I'd hold our stare like I used to. Instead I turn away, leaving your darkness disguised in crimson behind. Your words paint me the most lovely of art, but your actions set fire to it.

Opposition

He was silent as he crept away. Never would I have caught him, had he exited as quiet as the escape. But no, my love was not one for the shadows. He slammed the door swiftly, shaking my foundation, the very walls I existed between — just to make sure I knew he'd left.

Hinges

Six years with the door shut, isolated in a dull room you called friendship. You made sure I didn't notice the spikes growing from the desk, the bed of nails designed to pinch my back until it became raw. Only for so long, could I stand the stinging at the back of my throat from the sobs I swallowed to keep our peace.

The garden gleamed so colourful outside my window. How I wish it were me. It never crossed your mind that I was suffocating, trapped within your walls, whispering my pleads for air.

Outside, flowers bloomed from hope. So I crept through the cracks and planted myself in the caring grass, mended by the sun's rays.

I hope you think of me when you glance outside and see daffodils in the garden. We'll be waiting for your next corpse.

The Garden

It's been a while, you told me, standing in the place we began. The bench that resides at the bottom of the staircase screams for me to run up its steps, away from the boy who left me sobbing at its feet merely months ago.
Oh but it hasn't, not for me. I see you every night, drifting between my weak walls when the exhaustion sets in. Your crimson coat glows against the hushed tones of dusk, creeping between my eyelids until sorrow sets in.
Yeah, it sure has. Need I say more, my dear love? Distance has always been your delicacy. Quiet engulfed my affection until your eyes burned with fulfillment.
I miss you. Three words, the same ones that dragged me back into your gravity the last time.

I miss you, too.

Every so often, once in a blue moon, a situation will arise where you feel completely powerless. Hope is ripped from your subconscious and happiness is extinguished, put out as if it never lived there in the first place. During these times, no one can help you. You can't even help yourself, and to me? To me, that is the saddest, most fearful part of living.

Plea for help

I held my breath. Eyes closed in slow motion, then snapped back open. Oxygen couldn't reach my lungs, nor my brain, but it was okay, I was okay. It wasn't until my toes turned blue and spots appeared before me, after my knees buckled and the cold bath water erupted out of the eggshell tub. When my mother picked up the phone and sobs echoed through the quiet household, I knew it was over. He was gone.
A knock on the door. I wish I was, too.

Porcelain nightmares

The Greens

I've always admired the pine forest that rests atop the hill. Every winter, if braces itself for destruction, the needles right lord from its' branches and wind against its' back. But every spring, when the birds realize the chirps hiding in their throats may come out again, that the sun is trying to shine, the forest picks itself up again. It grows new roots in the place of old ones that no longer remain. The cycle repeats, over and over, but the forest stands tall and green and strong. Oh, how I wish I could do the same.

Re-planting

Today, I'm beginning to accept the body I've lived
in for these sixteen short years.

I look in the mirror and question what I saw wrong
yesterday, why the thought of my shape fueled my
self-hatred and despair just last week.

The number on the scale and pictures of others
much more fit or beautiful don't mean a single
thing.

Not when I am finally, after all this time,
able to say that I've come to terms with the shell
I've been hiding inside of,
when the tears are gone and there's nothing left but
a dull neutralness.

This is my day;
the one we've all been waiting for.

Acceptance

I knew not to chase after him. He had been the cause of my happiest days and of the opposite. Though I was unsure of the steps I'd need to take away from him, as I had only ever followed his careful footsteps, it was time that he knew I would not be there anticipating his return. I was no one's second choice, not even if I had begun as his first.

Footsteps

Seven days ago,
on the first Sunday of November,
I was a girl left crippled by the distaste of
a boy who never cared.

Sobbing, screaming, and broken,
I didn't know how to pick up the pieces when
my hands shook at the thought of him.

Today, though?
Today I am stronger.
I have lived as I was meant to,
created friendships I never thought I'd have,
and felt every emotion the dictionary could not
define.

In the wake of loss,
contentment and satisfactory acceptance of the
cards I've been dealt has become my companion.

Those who I thought I couldn't get back have
returned, better and happier and more
understanding.
And I truly do think that they are the reason
I am the woman I was not seven days ago.

Life, continued

For some reason, you have me mistaken for a dainty piece of string, capable of nothing unless you give me purpose. My love, how I bet you wish it were true? I will not stay wrapped around your finger, but I'll always leave a mark. Isn't that what forget me not's are for?

Forget me not

Sometimes a message is enough. Where has my stress gone? Well, it escaped in the shivers down my spine as I typed my worries away! It's alright, it had to be done, but still I wonder if my tone could've been altered in such a way that trapped the misery and loneliness before it could rise to the surface.

My troubles have gone!

"The poor thing, she had yet to find out that love and loss go hand in hand."

Lessons

Never mistake a boy with the moon in his eyes for sunshine. All his life he will chase things he cannot obtain, and you will be stuck following in his despondent footsteps. Though he may appear eager, he is in and out of your life as frequently as the changing tides.

Man In The Moon

Do not ever re-build a bridge that is meant to stay in pieces.

Poor Infrastructure

It's almost as if we were sedimentary rock;
each of the five a layer different from the next.
If one of us crumbled, the rest would lunge
forward and shake us from our fallen state.
As many times as you count the stars, it's as
many times as we could count on one another.

The Weenies

A Thank You....

First of all, I'd like to thank whoever has made it this far in my book. I hope that my words have resonated with you as so many wonderful authors have resonated with me and inspired the creation of Coloured Ink.

Thank you to my family, who I kept this project a secret from for many months. You have all supported me from the very beginning, and for that I'm immensely grateful.

Thank you to my friends and acquaintances, who push me to be the best version of myself, even in the wake of love, loss, and insecurity.

Thank you to my teachers, especially Mr. Pisterzi, who has encouraged growth in my writing since the day that scared, freshman girl walked into his classroom.

Thank you to the people that told me this would never happen. It was because of you that this was published.

Thank you to the muses of these poems. You may not know they are about you, or you may have figured it out as soon as your eyes skimmed my words. Either way, positive or negative, you all let me express my feelings towards you in the only way I knew how.

About the author;

Paige Pierce is a high school student on Vancouver Island, Canada. She began writing as a form of coping with the angst and hope that accompanies adolescence, then decided to publish her work after encouragement from the people close to her. Paige is planning on attending university in Vancouver, Canada after she graduates to become a Psychologist. Coloured Ink, her debut poetry anthology, was self-published in 2018, and more of Paige's work can be found online.

Printed in the USA
CPSIA information can be obtained
at www.ICGtesting.com
LVHW020744260124
769747LV00002B/356